The Dream Book

Also in this series:

The Good Spell Book
Love Charms, Magical Cures,
and Other Practical Sorcery

The Fortune-Telling Book
Reading Crystal Balls,
Tea Leaves, Playing Cards, and
Everyday Omens of Love and Luck

THE DREAM BOOK

DREAM SPELLS,
NIGHTTIME POTIONS
AND RITUALS,
AND OTHER MAGICAL
SLEEP FORMULAS

by

Gillian Kemp

ORION

In memory of
my mother, Ruth, who visits my
dreams with premonitions.
To Rosie Posy,
my Yorkshire terrier, and her
godmother Katie Boyle.
To my father, Mike, and
my sister, Alison.
Also to Sharon and to John.
To my publisher Mary
and her associate Jennifer.
To my agent Chelsey.
To my artist Julia.
To you the reader. And also
to the one I love.

Contents

Hold a book, close your eyes,
open a page, and put your
finger on it. Open your eyes
and begin reading from
where you pointed.
The words are premonitory.

*D*reams are teachers, designed to make our desires come true. They allow us to discover our true destinies by disclosing nature's secrets through the language of the soul. They are our subconscious and the essence of our being. Dreaming is a form of clairvoyance, because it gives us inner vision that can attune us to our souls and to purer, higher forces, revealing the truth. The study and interpretation of dreams is known as *oneiromancy,* and dates back centuries. *Oneiro* is Greek for dreams, and *mancy* is Greek for divination. Ancient Greeks and Egyptians, and biblical figures such as Moses, Pharaoh, and Joseph in the Old Testament changed the course of history by believing that their dreams were prophecies from God. ¶ We all dream, even babies and animals. The sleep of dreams is light and easily recognized by rapid eye movement called REM. We do not dream during deep sleep, in which there is no REM. Light sleep and deep sleep alternate throughout the night. Our deepest sleep occurs in the first hour and a half. After that, the brain moves into light sleep and dreaming begins. We dream for about two hours a night, which adds up to several years over a lifetime. We do not sleepwalk during dreaming, because messages from the brain cause a natural limb paralysis. Just as a sleep-walker can "see" where he or she is walking with his or her eyes closed, so can a person whose spirit leaves the body during a dream "see" his or her body asleep with the body's eyes closed. What we "see" in a dream is the pictorial incarnation of creative thoughts. Your soul has superior, intuitive foresight and insight beyond the limitations of conscious thoughts and views. If you are lucky, you may even see visions at your bedside after waking. Such visions are called "dream traces" and disperse at your slightest movement. ¶ We are all able to receive prophecies, because dreams awaken us to our souls. Dreams that come true are proof of the soul's existence. The soul subconsciously receives supernatural pictures, words, and messages. Once your mind is focused on the phenomena of dreaming as a real experience, another, higher consciousness of the supernatural develops, because dreams are the language of the subconscious. ¶ Both past and future can be seen in dreams because dreams enable a person to make contact with his or her deepest aspirations and wishes, which are often subconsciously submerged. Dreams are wonderful problem solvers that tidy up and separate material differently than the conscious mind does. The subconscious mind presents dramatic symbols and exaggerated likenesses to attract our attention to problems. Dreams allow us to face problems while we sleep, so that when we wake up, we can solve conundrums the conscious, reasoning mind has failed to solve. The solution to a problem usually appears at the end of a dream, but sometimes a series of dreams brings the solution. Other dreams show the consequences of problems we may not consciously be aware of having. In some dreams, we imagine that a problem is solved, such as when we imagine we are awake but are actually still asleep because at that moment sleep is preferable. ¶

Dreams can speak in parables, analogies, and symbols already affiliated with the dreamer's mind, interpretation, and unique emotions. Different types of dreams serve different purposes. Dreams can be prophetic, giving a glimpse of what we can expect to happen in our immediate and more distant future. We can also "visit" living or dead loved ones in our dreams, and send and receive telepathic messages during sleep. Through dreams, we can discover the truths hidden by sleeping loved ones by speaking to them while they are asleep. All of this and more will be revealed in this magical dream book.

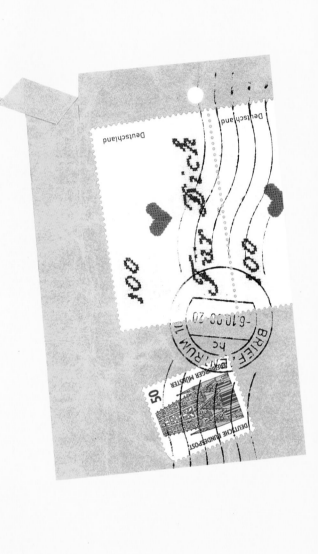

The five types of Dreams

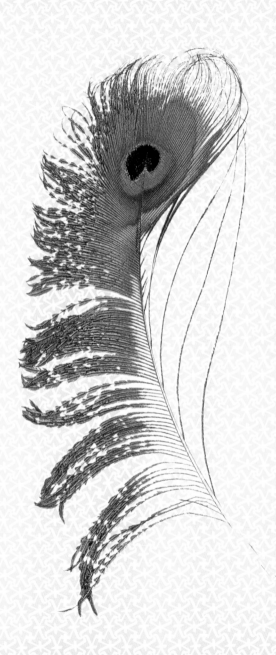

There are five different types of dreams: ordinary, lucid, telepathic, premonitory, and nightmare. They often blend and merge with one another.

ORDINARY DREAMS

During the day our conscious minds are active, but at night the subconscious takes over. Ordinary dreams are based on the activity of the unconscious in response to what we have seen or heard in our waking hours. Even a single thought can trigger a dream. Automatic unconscious stores of knowledge that have made an impression remain filed in the brain and unperceived until "read" by dream symbols, which are "the language of the soul." Events of the day and from years past are mirrored in the sleeping mind, as seemingly long-forgotten memories can resurface in dream imagery. The soul is particularly susceptible to the bygone memories that are brought to light through pictures in the mind's eye. In addition to being clairvoyant, dreams are also clairaudient, as we hear souls speak in our minds' ears. *Clairvoyance* means "clear sight." It is the supernatural ability to see people and events far away in time or location. *Clairaudience* means clear hearing. It is the faculty to hear with the mind's ear. Words spoken to us in our dreams should be taken literally, because such spiritual communication can show us how we should be when awake. You can get the best out of your future by understanding what a dream is saying to you pictorially and verbally.

LUCID DREAMS

A lucid dream is one that you can control because you are aware that you are dreaming. You can also decide what to dream about before going to sleep and then dream about the very thing that you planned to.

TELEPATHIC DREAMS

Telepathy, known as "the language of the angels," allows the dead and the living to speak in dreamland. In this meeting place, death is no barrier, and the living cross the threshold into a heavenly sphere of existence. This mental communication can also occur mind-to-mind between two living people. We may send our own or receive others' intentional or unintentional thoughts as mental visions in dreams. Extended telepathy during sleep is a communion between two worlds, the night-time world of the soul and the daytime world of the body.

PREMONITORY DREAMS

Premonitory dreams are similar to telepathic dreams in that your spirit leaves your body and ventures on a voyage of discovery. Premonitory dreams are special because they reveal the future and allow the dreamer to see truths that are not accessible in waking life. In tele-pathic dreams, we can also detect information about an imminent event. Dreams are the catalyst that put your body into motion to follow and fulfill your wishes and desires.

NIGHTMARES

Most nightmares are linked to early childhood, when we are inexperienced and therefore dependent on others. Before the age of three, we have not yet developed a sense of conscience and of right and wrong. Nightmares are representations of a suppressed, original fear commonly created by excessively strict parental or sibling moral standards and the threat of punishment in the face of innocence.¶ In nightmares you may perceive a warning for yourself or for a loved one. To be forewarned is to be forearmed: if you first see a frightful event in a dream, you can prevent harm from happening in waking life. For example, nightmares can warn against acting on impulse, as well as show that certain feelings and emotions are unhealthy.¶ Not all nightmares are nasty predictions or unwholesome signs. A nightmare may also relate to an old, unsolved problem that is so frightening to face that we are unable to continue to dream and the emotional terror wakes us in distress without offering a solution.

105 Queenstown's Cathedral on Hill Above the
Harbor—Ireland.

Recurring dreams

It is said that your wish will
be granted if you count nine
stars in the sky and make a wish.
Count the same stars or
another set of nine stars on eight

$\mathcal{R}$ecurring *dreams* release repressed emotions and focus our attention on unsolved problems. Their aim is to restore our personalities back to complete, undamaged health. Some past experiences show where a problem originated but appear only in fragments. If we are scared to face a problem, we wake in fright or forget the dream that we just had. The same or a similar dream then recurs, presenting new versions and exaggerations until the message is understood and the cause of the problem is dealt with. Each time the dream is repeated, subconscious memory and imagination about the future merge further, improving our thoughts and actions until they finally suggest a solution. Even though each of us is unique, many people share the same recurring dreams.

BEING CHASED

This is a common dream in which the dreamer is often rooted to the spot, unable to move. The dream is a sign of anxiety and lack of confidence. It may relate to childhood, when you lacked the physical power to run away from a frightening experience, or to infancy, when you lacked the ability to walk. To be able to run when pursued in a dream reveals your wish to be wooed and also prophesies your successful achievement of personal ambitions and long-held desires.

more consecutive nights. After nine nights in total, your wish will begin to come true.

BEING NAKED
IN PUBLIC

Nudity uncovers a desire to express yourself and to be less self-conscious and secretive. If in your dream you find yourself inhibited and fearing public disapproval, this points to your frustration and difficulty in being yourself. Perhaps in childhood you were punished for seeking attention, causing you to grow up self-conscious and lacking confidence.

BEING UNPREPARED
FOR AN EXAM

To dream of being unprepared for an exam reveals a fear of failure in a current challenge. The subjects that you dream about may be questions on an exam in waking life.

CLIMBING

To see yourself climbing a ladder, a hill, or any other object shows an ambitious desire to make it to the top and is an omen that you are on your way to achieving your lofty enterprise. You may need to push yourself onward and upward to reach your desire. You will succeed if you reach the top in the dream.

It is said that to turn your

DINING WITH A PRESIDENT
OR CELEBRITY

To dream of dining with a VIP denotes a subconscious urge to gain admittance to a higher society. It can also be a premonition that you will be mixing in elevated social circles.

FALLING

Fear of failure is revealed by a dream of falling or being afraid of falling. You may be afraid of a moral decline or a lapse in ambition or business. You may be driving yourself too hard trying to reach a goal. It may also be a premonition that precedes an avoidable setback or loss. Expect good fortune if you fall in a dream without being hurt.

[25]

FLYING

Flying represents a longing for freedom and a wish to escape constraints. It can also be a sign that you will transcend troubles and soar to great heights above and beyond the limits of your expectations, receiving praise along the way.

mattress on Sunday is a sign that you will lose your lover.

LOSING SOMETHING

Dreaming of losing something indicates insecurity about the lost object. It may be a premonition, in which case the loss can be avoided with your diligent care.

MEETINGS

When we dream of partaking in an activity with some-one we know, that person is in the back of our minds, whether he or she is alive or dead.

MEETING THE DEAD

To dream of someone who has died means that you had a real meeting with that person, and his or her spirit is alive and well. This person has had a loving influence on you in life and will keep giving you help by meeting you in your dreams.

MEETING STRANGERS

We all encounter strangers in our dreams whom we nei-ther know nor recognize. Whether the dreamer is male or female, an unknown woman or girl can represent our intuitions or a personification of the female personality. Men or boys in dreams, also irrespective of the gender of the dreamer, can reflect an inner masculine character. This is based on animus/anima (male/female), the principle that everyone has both a male and a female personality in his or her emotional makeup.

MISSING A PLANE OR TRAIN

A plane or train journey represents your personal journey through life. To miss either unveils a frustration at being unable to find your vocation or path in life, or to make as much progress as you would like. You may be too fearful to keep going forward. If in future dreams you catch the train, you will know that you are on the right track, have found your niche and achieved something.

[27]

OBJECTS COMING TO LIFE

A common object that comes to life in dreamland is a toy. This dream is a sign that you are maturing. You may be discovering new interests in subjects that you were once indifferent to, such as sports, music, religion, academics, art, or romance.

SWIMMING

Swimming reveals that your subconscious is encouraging you to attain your goal. The difficulty or ease with which you swim reflects how hard or simple your aim to achieve "the shore" will be. It may also relate to a birth trauma or the fear you experienced in learning how to swim.

Bad Dream Superstitions

- "To dream of things out of season
  Is trouble without reason."

- To dream of a wedding, a white bird, or broken glass precedes someone's demise.

- It is bad luck to tell someone your dream before breakfast.

- To dream that a ring falls off your finger is an omen that you will lose a friend

- To dream of losing a tooth is a sign that you will quarrel with a friend.

Keeping a dream Diary

Dreams have an elusive quality and are spirited away into the ether as mysteriously as they come. The secret to remembering them lies in recalling dream components precisely at the moment when your dream begins to slip away, as you vaguely begin to move from the ethereal twilight world to the waking state. The best time to write a dream down is before even getting out of bed. For this purpose, buy yourself a hardback notebook that will become your personal prediction book. Don't allow yourself to wake up completely until you have cast your mind back and willed yourself to consciously and concisely remember your dream. Force yourself to recall objects, locations, conversations, and actions, as well as colors.¶ In your dream diary, write the date of your dream and whether you felt happy or disturbed about what you saw. Next, write or draw the sequence of your dream or dreams. If you remember only fragments, note those objects or remnants that you can remember. Since dreams are pictorial, you may find it easier to draw pictures as you saw them rather than interpreting your dreams into words. If conversations occurred, write those down too. Finally, under the heading "Prediction," hazard a guess as to how and when you think your dream will come true.¶ Once you begin to collect dreams, you will see that dreams do come true, whether they are inspired by beneficial spirits or by your own subconscious. Dreams are personal and related to your unique problems and experiences. You may see a pattern emerge where certain recurring personal emblems or verbal messages always precede good or misfortune that is then repeated in your waking life. This fixed symbolism will give you a common language for interpretation.¶ At the very least you will see your dream as coincidental or as a previously rehearsed play. Some dreams may encourage you to follow an ambition by revealing the outcome, but may not necessarily show you what you have to go through or how long it will take to achieve. This can be good, as it prevents you from changing your mind about a course of action.

DREAM DIARY KEYS

When a dream comes true, tick it off in your book or draw a line underneath it and note the date. Write how your prediction matches what happens in your waking life. Perhaps stick matching colored stars or use corresponding numbers to link your premonition with your dream come true. You could use the first half of your diary for dream predictions and the second half for dream fulfillment. You could also have an "In-and Out-Tray" section for problems discovered and problems solved. Your dream magic book is unique to you.¶ The strange imagery of dreams is reciprocal, made by your imagination from within and from without, like breathing. To dream freely, your psyche must be free rather than inhibited or limited by your desires or fears when making predictions. Only then can your sight have true clairvoyance.¶ Your interpretation of the time for when an event might occur may be right in one way but wrong in another. Only when the event actually occurs in your waking life will you see how the timing of your dream was right but slightly different than what you expected.¶ As your dreams emerge and are recorded in your dream diary, your clairvoyance will naturally develop into a deeper, richer, more colorful and more audible experience. You will gain a stronger understanding of your own psyche and your personal rapport with higher forces that gently guard, guide, heal, and help you, revealing the way while you simply sleep.

33

Good Dream Superstitions

- "Friday's dream Saturday told Is bound to come true, however old."

- You will have "the luck of the devil" if you dream of the devil.

- To cry in a dream foretells coming joy and prosperity.

- To dream of a funeral is a sign of a wedding.

- To dream of a death is an omen of birth.

- To dream of music is a portent of a speedy marriage.

A~Z

dream dictionary

Зоологическ